# WANDERINGS:

## A Continuation Of My Journey

*by*

## Helen Napoli Cabrera

Printed by MJM Graphic Communications in the United States of America

Visit www.cabrera44.com to order book

# WANDERINGS:

## A Continuation Of My Journey

by

Helen Napoli Cabrera

11.30.10
Dear Glen –
Your smile
is great!
Love,
Helen

MJM Press

June, 2005

*I have just finished reading the edited manuscript of this book.  Sitting with my cup of tea and the morning sun, I seem to be removed from the text as the writer and have experienced the wanderings as one who just opened a new book (just as you are doing now) from my shelf! I pray that you experience the essence of this book, as I have just done, and realize that your grief and pain have been felt by another.  To know that you will survive to find happiness, again, is what  you must  believe. The sun is shining into my window; may it find you wherever you are. As our minister shares with his congregation every Sunday:* **Go Enjoy!**

*HNC*

# Contents

# Welcome to Wanderings:
## A Continuation Of My Journey.

Wanderings seems to capture where I am at this time in my life. It is a wandering from place to place, from situation to situation. When my husband died, September 30, 1997, the planning and pleasure we had together ceased. Now I wander and wonder.

*Wanderings:*      timeless travels, meanderings. The dictionary helps pinpoint the essence of my journey. I agree with timeless travels (because time is now less important than it had been before) and meanderings give me a quietness that enables me to see and feel all that touches me. Even the wind receives special attention!

This second phase of my journey shares with you places and people who touch me on this gest. Everyday I feel and see a new dimension to the ordinary, to the everyday comings and goings that surround me. I take time to feel and enjoy.

Come with me. Experience the continuation of my journey of remembering yesterday, celebrating today and anticipating tomorrow.

If you have also lost your loved one, may you feel my reflections, my trying to understand and my need to go on within the pages of this book. Grief does lift enough for you to continue living; please have hope.

*HNC*

## Chapter I - October 1, 2000
## My Wanderings Begin

**Reaching September** happened. Three years have passed since Jim's death. It was the beginning of football season and our grandsons were excited about their first game. I remembered other Septembers and wrote. Poetry, or even journal entries, will give you an outlet for those inner thoughts. When seeing them on paper, reading what you have written, closing your eyes, feeling your loss, knowing you can visualize your memories with words and thoughts; this enables you to go on. Jim's face and Melville's quote came together in my mind's eye and I was able to be at peace. When Tyler shared with me that Moby Dick was his favorite book, Melville's quote took on a more special meaning as I embraced the grandchild that looks so much like my Jim.

"And there is a Catskill eagle in some souls that can alike dive down into the blackest gorges, and soar out of them again and become invisible in the sunny spaces. And even if he forever flies within the gorge, that gorge is in the mountains; so that even in his lowest swoop the mountain eagle is still higher than the other birds upon the plain, even though they soar."

HERMAN MELVILLE, Moby-Dick

## Reaching September

When September arrives and
It is September,
I am reminded of another September:
The September of his death.

The months preceding that September
Were filled with pain and emotion.
He was going to die before October dawned.
I held onto the hope that September would never end.

My hope, his bravery,
My love, his response,
My sadness, not to be shared.
My hand holding his.

Our family, there for him.
His awareness of our love,
Passion expressed for getting well.
Quiet times, just us two.

September did not signal the approaching Fall.
My focus was singular.
The outside world had no impact.
I thought only of yesterdays.

Today, when September arrives
I think about other Septembers.
Septembers that were,
And, Septembers that will be.

You will relate to the following poems if your loss has caused you to ask these very questions of yourself. Know that I have felt these pressing emotions and you can find contentment, just try.

**Lonely vs. Alone** is a product of a wandering mind, not body. I have reached another plateau and with it arrived fear. **Grief Alias Fear** was penned. **When Is It My Turn?** was a frustrated plea until the answer was found. Wanting to experience today and all tomorrows without the terrible pain of loss, looking toward others became necessary. **Hope** was found in poetry form as two friends (Anne and Henry) married after the death of their spouses (David and Connie).

### Lonely vs Alone

Lonely is your dependent friend,
Alone is your independent ally.
They are words that we hear,
Phrases we constantly resort to:
"I'm all alone,"
"I am very lonely,"
Without understanding the words,
Without truly dissecting the phrases.

Lone is strong and brave:
The Lone Star State, for example.
Add an ly and strength and bravery flee!
Bobby Vinton's: Mr. Lonely.
"No one to phone,
No one to touch,"
A sometimes desperate image.
Lonely, not wanting to be alone.

Why?

Alone is a wonderful place to be.
It is a time to hug yourself.
Enjoy your accomplishments.
No negative space between the letters.
It is tightly wound around who you are.
Alone you can talk to yourself, ideas abound.
Alone you can remember the best.
Alone you can dream without interruption.
Alone you can be you!

Who are you?

You are both independent and dependent.
That is who we all are.
A plethora of feelings.
Feelings we need to share,
A need to communicate, at times dependent.
Feelings kept for our quiet minutes,
Alone, happy and independent.

You **can** and **will** choose.

Sometimes it is difficult to be alone,
We need others, but choose carefully
So that we are not lonely.
For we can be alone in a crowd,
Enjoying every minute.
Or, lonely in a group,
Wanting not to be so, lonely.

What is the answer?
Can you find an answer?
Yes, within **you**.
You must select the feeling:
Lonely or alone.
You must be strong.
You must be happy.
You must try harder to understand yourself.
You will find treasures galore!

For **You** can be alone and not lonely.

## Grief Alias Fear

Grief rears its head,
How to handle its arrival.
You know why:  a loss.
Your being alone is here and now.
But is it **FEAR**?  Yes, no,
Yes, I am fearful.

Fearful of being without a partner,
An overwhelming responsibility.
Always having shared the load,
Now the burden is mine.
No one to speak your thoughts to,
Your tomorrows appear bleak.

Is there now a fear for my death?
No, that fear seems not with me.
Probably age and faith have helped.
I have lived a death and felt grief,
But fear, no.

Never fearful as to financial stability,
Thank God.
My health prognosis, today, causes no fear,
Thank God.
No fear of the extent of my ability,
Thank God.

What fear then?
I know in the depths of thought
I fear:  loneliness.
To be alone at night is fearful.
The loss of being touched.
Being by myself and ill,
Absence of a two-way conversation,
No one to care for, to care for me,
No eyes to look at you over meals,
Never a good night kiss,
No one to see your tears,
To hear your laughter,
A list of omissions.
Grief is fearful.

It arrives on a good bye.
It stays with you in the dark,
You cannot rid yourself of it in daylight.
It marches with you and your drummer.
It causes anxiety and endless running.
It cannot be denied.
It blankets the sun.
It destroys ambition.
It eliminates dreaming.
It isolates you.

Yes, fear is your worst enemy while grieving.

Call it by its name:  **FEAR.**
Do not camouflage it with another name.
Fear must be overcome.
It is an unwelcome companion
Fear not; see it for what it is:

The loss of hope.

So,

See the sun,
Feel its warmth,
Reach out and touch,
With your hands and your voice.
Care with all your heart.
Help as only you can.
View tomorrow as an adventure.
Fear not, for your hope is with you.
You are alive!

### When Is It My Turn

As I sit and ponder my day,
I oft times ask
"When is it my turn?"
I have given what I can.
I have shared all I have.
Agonized over others,
Tried my best, so:

When will I have others care about me?
When will it be my turn?

Take a walk, clear your head.
Are you being selfish, wanting?
Do I administer with a hook,
Do for me if I do for you?
No strings attached to my caring.
Is that true, or just boastful?
Can I give and not receive?
Love and not be loved in return?

I realize I cannot make you love me,
But, when will it be my turn?

I sow, can I not also reap?
Why am I not included, when I include?
Why am I not considered, when I am considerate.
Smile at me, with me,
My smile is meant to warm you.
I love and care in order to be.

I ponder, I wish, I want.
I must stop my wanting and look about.

I see a wheelchair:
I guess it was not my turn as I walk away.
I read an obituary:
My name does not appear, not my turn.
The pain of loss touched another:
I have missed another turn!

*Imagine, not wanting another's turn.*

*I realize it is my turn*
*At living*
*At sharing*
*At helping*
*At caring*
*At loving*
*At success.*

*The joy of having a turn is what is beautiful.*
*Your turn makes you happy!  Not another's.*
*You must reach out and not expect a "return".*

*Your turn is everyday:*
*At getting up*
*At having breakfast*
*At feeling your nose*
*At seeing a flower*
*At touching a friend*
*At buying a present*
*At sharing a thought*
*At walking to a special place*
*At breathing freedom*
*At feeling no pain*
*At thinking*
*At understanding*
*At creating.*

*So I YELL:*

**"My Turn!"**


*(for Luis)*

## Hope

What a beautiful day!
Perfect day for a wedding.
What a beautiful church!
Perfect place for a wedding.
What a beautiful bride!
Perfect for the groom.
Yes, perfect in every way.

The bride's bouquet of lilies of the valley,
The participation of family,
Children, grandchildren in Sunday dress.
Friends and in-laws, to be and have been,
Await a special service of marriage.
"Special in what way?", you ask.
Special because hope is present.

Flashback and youth appears.
Happy in the ways of the young.
Babies and dreams,
Love and joy,
Accomplishment and tomorrows,
Days and nights together,
All bound with mutual respect.

Then God calls and all is gone.
"Not everything", you say.
I say, "Everything", loud and clear.
Tomorrows appear only to disappear.
Today does not exist.
Loneliness is a constant companion.

Where is hope?

Question why family is not enough.
Wonder why friends cannot fill the void.
Search for an hour when the pain will subside.
Sleepless nights find no answers.
Your tears are no longer soothing.
A need to mend becomes a beacon.

Reaching for hope is necessary.

Where can I find hope for happiness?
Will this loneliness subside?
How do I help myself?
Why is it so hard to go forward?
Let me read to find an answer.
Allow me friends who will listen.

Hope arrives through someone caring.

Another to talk with,
Someone who has been there,
A nod of understanding,
Touching.
Smiles of anticipation play at your mouth,
Embarrassed by your inability to stay mature,

Hope has entered your life, again.

This special day, this wedding day,
Family and friends rejoice.
Hope and love join you at the altar.
Flowers dedicated to those you still love
Decorate the church this May day.
When asked, "Who gives this woman"
Voices heard in reply, "We do"

Echo in this place as

Connie fixes Anne's train

And

David straightens Henry's boutonniere,

We all feel the **hope** of tomorrow.

## Chapter II
## Nature Becomes A Must

Before "getting on the road" I did a lot of wandering with nature. It was a linking to that which was alive and thriving in a world that asked nothing of me. No people, just the beauty and simplicity of life that was right there, no traveling necessary. Grief saps your energy and you are at times so tired. To combat this weariness seeing myself as a bird, as a part of the bustle of the pond; or, just viewing a rainbow, feeling the wind enabled me to rest. I needed to have faith in nature, faith in the living species that called out in the night, touched my cheek in a gale, and looked down at me from the sky. They were things I could believe in without much effort, for I was healing.

It is a wonder to believe and see and feel that you are a part of nature that you view. A dear young friend, Kelly Smith, viewed the nature around her with wonder as she valiantly fought to live. Her photography won her awards in Marblehead, Massachusetts. An example is found in "Kelly's Pond" with its blooming Lythrum.

In **The Pond** I am a bird; in **A Winter Rainbow** and **The Wind**, I am myself with nature. **The Grace Of Gliding** addresses the freedom found in flying. All of these departures from myself helped build the confidence needed to experience that which was ahead, I needed to rest.

*Kelly's Pond by Kelly Smith, Marblehead, Mass.* 2002

## The Pond

Above the water,
Atop a tree,
I sit quietly, watching.
My white wings unflapping.
My body at rest.

The Pond is alive.
Small fish dart back and forth.
Large fish define round spawning holes.
Birds swim and dive for food.
Birds fly and skydive for food.
Families paddle, a family swim.
High-stepping individuals viewed.

A society beneath my perch.
The everyday living seen.
Events of family visible.
Chores of surviving necessary.
Contentment, though wary.
Friends and enemies together,
In the Pond.

Around the Pond,
Squirrels scurry,
Land birds nest,
Snails crawl,
Turtles bask,
Frogs leap,
Reeds sway,
Flowers bloom.
Life as usual.

Hearing and seeing,
A voyeur at best.
My needs are different.
I am content not joining.
Alone and yet a part.
I must feed,
I must fly,
I cannot stay just perched.

Yet,

I need not socialize.
Family duties are no more.
I care for myself only.
The group needs not my counsel.
The Pond will survive without me.
Its beauty is forever.
I am not forever.

Perched high above the activity
I ponder on yesterday.
This day will end
Tomorrow's activities will commence
Necessity becomes paramount
To those living in, on and around the Pond.

And,

I will fly to the edge.
Acknowledge their lives.
Contribute where I can.
Answer their questions,
When asked.
Then, I must retire again
To the treetop and view

**The Pond.**

## A Winter Rainbow

What do I see?
Can it be?
Is it a mirage?
No, there it is.

A winter rainbow!!

On December eighteenth
When snow should be my companion
A rainbow appears in the winter sky
And I wonder at its chilled beauty.

The colors are truly frosty.
I see:
Cool green
Slicker pink
Icy blue
Alaska yellow.

The rainbow is not defined,
The colors fade into one another.
I see no purple,
Orange is not on the palette.

As I travel North, the colors change.
I see:
Christmas red,
Pine needle green,
Silent Night blue
Star-light yellow.

The grey sky is a backdrop.
Its color enhances the scene.
The clouds cause imagination.

The road becomes congested.
I am distracted and when I return
I see:
A winter sky.
I remember:

## A Winter Rainbow

*A place for your thoughts............*

## The Grace of Gliding

In Chapel this Sunday morning, listening,
The sermon reaching my ears,
While watching the pond and a crane on wing,
Their beauty touching my imagination.

My yearning for free flight envisioned.
My desire to travel without great effort.
To use God's wind to guide me.
To let my wings rest.

Gliding is graceful.
No abrupt motions to cause unfocusing.
No need for formation,
Just a peaceful performance.

Does gliding take place before the end of a journey?
Is it part of every flight?
Must you see your destination before you can glide?
Is it innate, or can you learn?

I see a hummingbird working so hard to become stable.
I visualize a soaring eagle.
I hear the flap of fowl in formation as they fly the sky.
Only the single gliding of a crane touches my tomorrow.

Instinctively I know the energy needed to become airborne,
Having expended that force to take off.
It was fueled by youth,
Interest and desire appeared on the horizon.

The flight was wonderful and gratifying,
Feeling my wings doing what I knew they could.
Meeting others flying to their own music,
I hummed along, tho' I had a theme song of my own.

Landing in places that were new,
I do not remember gliding.
It was always with self-power, jet speed,
Not the pace for gliding.

Was it graceful?
I found the flutter of wings beautiful.
Seeing the wingspread of flight, different spans,
A wonder, as we traveled the skyways.
But is it, was it, graceful?

As I find a need to glide,
Sometime from weariness,
The motion of the past forgotten,
My need to accomplish,
To execute that landing,
With style and grace,
Gliding becomes a goal.

My ego leads me to believe that others watched my flight.
Maturity evaporates the wanting to be watched.
I now know that others did not watch,
  nor did they always judge.
It was my flight, my sky-borne journey.

So, glide I must.
In true form, mine.
I see the blue sky, the white clouds,
The waters trapped so that I can land,
Past the trees, smell the flowers,

Glide to a landing.
Gracefully done!

(Was anyone watching?)*

*Maturity will arrive soon!

## The Wind

Hurricanes, tornadoes and cyclones.
Breezes, gusts and zephyrs.
Gentle, never-stopping, forceful.
The essence called Mariah.

Her origin is unknown to me,
She seems to originate during March,
To blow a whole year through.
A part of everyday life.

On a lazy day she moves the clouds.
A frenzy-filled day shakes the trees.
Ripples on a lake, her calling card.
Indecision causes gales and lulls.
Invisible to our eye,
Awareness on our skin,
As her smell is a plethora of scents.
Always aware of her presence or absence.

Her traveling partners are often seen:
Snowflakes, rain drops and hail.
Touch them, can we feel her?
We reach for her as she roughs our hair,
We come away empty-handed.
Turn and view her as we hear her approaching,
There is naught to see.
We cannot grasp a wisp within our fingers,
As our breath is taken away by this force.

The force, the wind.
Measured in knots, MPH.
How do you clock something not visible?
How do we harness an energy?
Our windmills know the answer,
Yet, I wonder.

In my searching, my wondering,
The wind becomes my metaphor.
I wonder at feeling the invisible,
Wonder at the existence of the unexplainable.
The wind is invisible and unexplainable;
Therefore, I believe the invisible and unexplainable exist.

Believing is continuing.
Understanding is believing.
Faith is believing you understand.
Comfort is found in faith.
Happiness is feeling comfort.

As the wind:
Rocks my hammock,
Blows milkweed whirligigs to seed,
Sculptures the clouds,
Helps or hinders the tides,
Cools my face,
I find a feeling of awesome comfort.

Comfort in my ease
At accepting that which I cannot hold.
Allowing life to flow as a river,
From its source to its mouth.
I also reach fulfillment at day's end,

Faith evolves.


(My 68th birthday)

## Chapter III
## Tasting Nature

My honeysuckle thoughts are all wrapped up with my time wandering as a youth. My Mother taught my sister and me to chain violets and wild daisies while we feasted on honeysuckle. There is always room for **A Drop Of Honey**.

On the path of life you may come upon a mulberry tree, as I have over these many years. At the age of six I found mulberries! My cousin had a white mulberry tree in her front yard and my uncle would help us harvest the fruit. Because we were too short to reach and too young to climb, he would place white sheets around the tree, shake the tree until the berries fell and we would consume. What fun! It was years later that I became *proficient* at picking a mulberry!

Sharing with you **How To Pick A Mulberry**, my only suggestion: if you are wandering in your Sunday best, choose a white mulberry, for the black mulberries are stainers!

## A Drop Of Honey

My sneakers falter on the loose sand
My glasses shield the sun
My sweater flaps in the wind
A walk in progress.

View the silhouette of New York City
Hear the gentleness of the waves
Feel the salty air
One step at a time, a walk.

The beat of a walking rhythm
In time with the beat of my heart
The need to fulfill a promise
To exercise, to walk.

Turn the corner, watch my step
Keep up the pace
Remember my objective:
A walk to be well.

What is that smell?
No, don't stop, I am on a roll!
Must stop, memories crowd.
I see them,

Honeysuckle.

Stop my feet, my swinging arms
Reach up and touch
Breathe deeply their fragrance,
Enjoy.

The years fall away
No need to walk then
I was always running
But I stopped to taste

The drop of honey.

Pick a blossom,
Hold it tenderly.
Snap off the bottom and separate.
Pull the pistil to the end:

A drop of honey.

Between my lips
On my tongue
Memory of youth
Time was mine,

As I stopped to taste

**A drop of honey.**

*Share a childhood memory.*

## How To Pick A Mulberry

First, find a mulberry tree and
Rejoice.
Check to see if the fruit is ripe and
Rejoice.
Smell the fragrance of the sweet fruit and
Rejoice.
Don't rejoice to loudly or people will
Stare!

Position yourself on the backside of a limb.
Look up and appraise the color of the fruit.
If the tree produces black mulberries,
Look for very dark berries.
If it is a white mulberry tree,
The berries are almost translucent.

Ready!

Reach up and touch.
If it releases from the limb easily,
It is ripe!
Pop it into your mouth quickly,
And reach for another.
Don't yearn for the juiciest you cannot reach!

Satisfaction can be found in one
Better still, a half dozen at once!!
Pick with both hands.
Savor each mouthful.
Enjoy to your hearts content,

For it is **Mulberry Picking Time**!!!
Time for purple fingers
Time for a purple tongue
Time for the sweetness of white
Time to remember that mulberry tree,

The one that taught you the joy of:

Mulberry picking!

*Mulberries*
*Copyright....Miriam Adams 2004*

# Chapter IV
## Hand-in-Hand with Other Women

*My Journey, The Loss Of A Loved One* found me questioning who I was and what my marriage taught me. The realization of my importance to my family was a bottom line item: a wife and mother. Now that my grown sons need only my love and my husband is gone I find my role as a mother and wife totally different. The mothering was due to become different, but I could no longer be a wife. Holding onto the part of me that would remain the same became paramount. I was still a woman.

Women. By remembering and observing there was a feeling of respect and belonging. I was a part of them. **Ava** had to be written because during a conversation about movie stars and the name Ava Garner was mentioned, these younger women queried: "Ava who?". **The Vermont Females** is a trilogy about young women starting their journey, women I observed. **The Waters of Women** gave notice to the grief of so many widows. **My Friend** helped me cope with losing, yet not losing, a special person. **On The Wings Of A Dragonfly** was my way of reaching out to a dear friend, Nancy, who had lost her daughter, Kelly, a brave, courageous woman. **A Penny For Your Thoughts** and **Eulie** were written about two women who stood out as strong individuals, women to admire.

I am now ready to continue my wanderings as a woman.

*Write about a woman you admire.*

## Ava

She was like a smoky drink.
Her eyes were sultry
Her voice low and calling
Her body echoed a need
Her talent rose above the image.

I will always remember her name:

Ava.

I wanted to dye my blonde hair,
Chestnut waves a must.
Change my name.
Practice her walk,
Most often without shoes.
She was naughty.

On the flip side I also wanted to be Doris.
Day after Day her movies made me dream.
Loved her neatness, her clothes,
Her perky roles, Rock Hudson.
Emulating her easy,
Emulating Ava would cause my parents alarm!

Then it happened:  SHOWBOAT.

She sat on the deck,
Her heart broken,
Her very soul crying out for
Her Bill.
She was all woman and I loved her.

Three hankies, not Kleenex,
Her soulful song echoing into the tides,
The river moving along and not caring.
Her beauty took your breath away.
Her unhappiness my teenage banner.

Ava will always be my special memory.
I believe she touched me because that was her.
Her personal habits caused sadness.
Loves could not tolerate her pain.
Her beauty could not compensate for her.

Maybe her beauty was her curse.
 The system demanded much.
Her public demanded more.
Her loves asked for part of her,
She was not able to share.

This was the legacy I received from **Ava**.

Fantasy or reality
The movie screen became the storyteller.
The lines read and made believable,
The darkness of the theatre,
The imagination of youth.

A vision for eternity,
A vision for me to reflect upon.
I wish to remember that woman,
That woman who lived and died in London.

My wish:  That she still walks barefoot.

## The Vermont Females I

The view from a bagel shop booth
Onto a strip mall
A long trip completed,
Vermont, I have arrived.

Sitting with her back to the wall
Self-consciously peering at the world
Not aware of my staring
Just waiting for family or friends.

Her fifteen plus years budded her tee.
The inherited curl pulled severely into a rubber band.
No makeup to cover freckles still accepted.
Pale lipstick on pouted lips, braces maybe?

Jeans, of course.
Then the L.L.Bean Wellingtons.
They shod her feet with loud acclaim.
In their bleak olive, loudly proclaiming:
I am me!

Then I notice the fingers eating french fries,
A little unkempt.
But, from mouth to throat, in a quick motion,
They stroked the piece de resistance,
A strand of luminous pearls.

The mark of the girl from **Bennington**.

## The Vermont Females II

I was there for a cone of soft ice cream
She was there to be with friends.
Three girls sitting atop picnic benches
At a roadside stand in **Bristol**.

Her smile and easy manner were electric.
Her shiny cropped blonde hair swayed as she laughed.
Her face was beautiful in an athletic clean way.
Her body liquid and easy.

I watched at she listened and quietly answered.
The dialogue was teenage and brilliantly empty.
Horseplay the ultimate body language.
Dress was high school team tee and black short shorts.

Sitting, bare legs into platform sandals, 3 inches at best.
Admiring her looks, her demeanor, her coordination,
She turned and smiled at me, sensing my perusal,
She stood to go and unfolded at least 6 feet 4 inches of beauty.

I watched in amazement, never realizing the height.
Never aware of anything other than her self image,
She moved with dignity and no embarrassment.
A reflection of ancestry that measures 3 inches more, her choice.

She ambled across the road with her friends,
Towering above yet fitting in.
Confident were her strides, one to their two.
Her destination this evening unknown to me.

I felt a slight bond, female to female.
Young woman, be always so proud.
Show it in your carriage
Express it in with laughter.

Enjoy.

*The Vermont Females  III*

**Middlebury**, *a town of college influences.*
*Her buildings, her presence.*
*Having lunch outside, I felt it all.*
*I was feeding my mind and body.*

*Then I fed my female ego.*
*She was a vision of herself.*
*As she came towards me*
*I registered every detail.*

*Her walk was made sturdy by her walking boots,*
*Thick walking socks billowed from the top.*
*The color of her cargo walking shorts and cotton top*
*The color of newly turned earth.*

*Her arms swung in time to her gait,*
*Determined and directed.*
*Her skin had darkened from the sun,*
*That same sun had come to rest in her hair.*

*For there nestled atop the swinging chestnut mane*
*A chain of newly woven daisies.*
*Worn, not with a girlish smile, but*
*With an aura of focus and destination.*

*This female of **Middlebury** was on a walk.*

## The Waters of Women

They lap every shore of this country,
The Atlantic, the Pacific, the Gulf.
Along the shore are seen their footprints,
Singularly marking the sands of time.

The rivers and streams are courted with their presence.
The slippery rocks and nettled underbrush
  complicate their trek.
They singularly move mountains of emotion
As they journey to death.

Offered are memories and hopes
One of yesterday, the other of tomorrow,
Only today seems to escape reality.
No room for **why me**? in their thoughts.

All sizes and all ages
A sameness is in their widowhood.
A sameness in their grief.
A sameness in the sadness of birthdays past.

They travel alone with their burdens.
Their eyes on the horizon, not on the ground.
They have not turned to dulling influences
Their bodies are alive and wanting.

Try, look around and see.
The waters you walk beside, let them comfort.
The colors of nature, feel their beauty.
You are you, a woman of sorrow, living to love.

Smile at those who pass,
Peruse nature and its creatures.
Your walk will reward you.
The waters will remind you,

So, cry, the waters of women.
Let them fall from your cheeks.
Run through your body,
Replenish the source of your pleasure,
The waters of this land, replenished with:

THE WATERS OF WOMEN.

## My Friend

She came to me from the North.
From snow and cold
To warmth and the Florida sun.

It has been a hard year,
She has been ill.
I have watched her struggle
With pride and aplomb.

These few days were wonderful.
We laughed, as I reminisced.
We talked, as I completed thoughts.
We shopped, as I remembered her zip code.
We dressed for church, what to wear?
We are girlfriends.

Thirty years devoted to our friendship.

A corporate partner to her husband,
Brilliant at best.
Her homes were warm and inviting,
Her daughters loved and cared for,
Her organizational skills sought after,
Her friendship valued.
Those unbelievable eyes, adored by her mate.
A life so productive.

Today, as she was driven to my house,
Those eyes and her hug welcomed me to her.
Contentment seemed the fare of the day,
My friend was with me again.
My grief at losing part of her faded.
Enjoyment filled every minute.

My friend had arrived.
I overlooked so much,
I imagined even more,
We were having a girl's weekend!
She was, thankfully, back with me.

Until,
I noticed, as she approached me.
She had her shoes on the wrong feet.

## On The Wings of A Dragonfly

Fly, soar and be free.
Let us not burden your flight
With our keening,
With our love,
With our yesterdays.

Your tomorrows are within your grasp.
Enjoy the weightlessness of the journey.
You have left us with more memories
Than can be told in a fortnight.
You will always be with us.

Gentle breezes will remind us:
emails from kelsmith33.

But, mostly, dear dragonfly, with:
A triumphant catch.
Hello hugs and smiles.
Hopeful and goodbye hugs and kisses.
Interest in a Nantucket morning.
A girlish prank.
A thank you note.
Love-stitched gifts.

Every step a child dances,
Every performance of a horse,
Every swish of a dog's tail,
Every soft purring of a cat,
Every spotting of a Kelly green item,
Every toss of hair by a willowy brunette,
Every time we look into a beautiful Irish face,
Every quiet moment,

You will be there, dear dragonfly.

We yearn to speak to you again.
To read and hear of your conquests,
Your ability to beat the odds,
To know you will read our latest letters,
To await your response.

All these are now beyond today.
We pray that tomorrow will ease the pain
The pain we felt today at the Olde North Church.
The open window, the tears, the stories,
The love and respect you so rightly earned.
They mark this day, dear dragonfly.

Memories all, a part of who you are.
Resting for just a moment,
As you soar into the ether.
Please fly well.

Enjoy the rainbows flashing on your wings.
Be excited for those tomorrows
Be content with the yesterdays.
Be yourself, no more is needed.

But, please, dear dragonfly,

Visit us often, for we miss you.

*Kelly Smith* *1964-2003*

### A Penny for Your Thoughts

She always was worth more than a Penny.
Gold on a good day,
Silver on a grey day.
She could be counted on to be valuable.
She was my friend.

Her counsel often sought.
Her comments straight forth.
Thoughtful always,
Truthful and caring,
Insightful and intelligent.
Her mind for you to search.
Her face for you to admire.

Organized to accomplish.
Focused on understanding.
Faith as a tool.
Penny faced every day with brilliance.
Always ready to enjoy life,
Always ready to include you.

Her beautiful hair a beacon.
Her smile joyful.
Her hands welcoming you,
A hug to comfort you.
Retiring in demeanor,
Exuberant in spirit.
Her presence always noted.
Quietly important,
She was my friend.

Along the Hudson,
In sunny Florida,
On the golf course,
Teaching an Alpha class,
Being a wife, mother, grandmother,
Bringing color into a room.
Done with grace and style,
Always a valued friend.

Her love for her family
Brought a smile to her lips,
Sparkles from her eyes.
Stories of events of importance,
A bit of wonder and pride,
They belonged to her.
They miss her.
They mourn their loss.

May our prayers comfort them.
May our shared memories bring joy.
May our sorrow bring warmth.
May we always show our friendship.
Today we share God's love, in this place,
In Penny's name.
As today slips into tomorrow,
We are thankful for the gift.
This most precious gift given to us,
For too short a time,
The gift:

That of knowing and loving Penny.

## Euli

You could not miss her,
She was robust and red-haired.
It was her presence.
It was her never being still.
It was her being in charge.
It was her knowing the answer,
To questions asked and not asked.
All these made you pay attention.

But,

It was her love of golf I will remember.

That is where I first met her,
 At the golf course:
As chairman of an event,
As a bustling volunteer,
As a fellow golfer,
In the winner's circle.

A winner she was.
Eight children to love.
Twenty-one grandchildren to spoil.
A happy marriage to embrace.
A career to be proud of.
A competitive spirit to rely on.
A caring soul to reach out.

And

A damn-good golf swing,

## Chapter V
### Dressing for my Wandering

Ready to "go". Traveling beyond nature and myself a must! Packing my bags and getting on the road because there are people to meet, places to see; but, what do I wear?

You need to know my love for beautiful clothes. During Jim's illness there was neither time nor desire to address my wardrobe. Still in my night clothes at 11:00 a.m., my sister, Ginny, took me aside and informed me of the need to keep things as normal as possible. Keeping appearances the same afforded me time for myself. It is not easy to find even "minutes" when you are stressed.

After Jim's death my closet became a focus of my attention. Shopping seemed to fill the hours of pain, probably because of the nature of shopping. It is a happy chore that you are able to plan, execute and find closure in a single afternoon. Of course not everyone puts that much emphasis on hanging things! I realized this and with tongue in cheek I immortalized my closet!

I laughed at **Closet Clothes** and then packed.

## Closet Clothes

They arrive without fanfare.
Well, maybe a little
Because the price was right,
The color was special
Even though it matched nothing.
Fantasy overrode logic,
Memories of yesterday's look,
The feel of soft fabric,
Paid for and packaged,

These closet clothes.

Some still boast the original tags.
Others are tired from being tried on.
They all are similar in one respect,
They rarely have left the closet.

Unless,

They were moved to winter storage,
Then aired out for summer use,

Or

They were moved to summer storage,
Then aired out for winter use.

Or

Unless,

Their presence was needed.

My, they are special.
I arrive to peruse their habitat.
I feel the fabrics and enjoy the colors,
What size?  Do they still fit?

At times I realize their age.
Have twenty years gone since they arrived?
Memories of events they attended,
Worn to special balls and parties,
They hang taller than their neighbors,
Laughter and companionship surround them.
Touch and remember.

I wonder if they miss being worn,
Almost as much as I miss those days.
They never answer my sighs,
They never look away as I ponder their plight,
For they must know,

After twenty years or more,

That they will remain,
Row after row,
Item after item,
Touched and passed over,

For yet, another year, or maybe more,

**My Closet Clothes!**

# Chapter VI
## Seeing and Feeling Color

I started to travel. I wandered and I saw. Driving alone to New Hampshire to visit friends I experienced **The Grey of Summer**. In Vermont it was a small town called Peru that inspired **A Special Time** and **The Moth**. At the foot of Mt. Abraham I penned **The Color Green** (my grandson, Peter, found all the shades of green in a box of Crayolas). There was the fixation with stone walls and a wonderful B & B in New Hampshire that inspired **Stone Walls and Stepping Stones**.

## The Grey of Summer

Where did the rainbows go?
What has become of the sparkle?
The images on the water are no more.
The warmth of summer turned to chill.

All I see is grey from blue eyes that seek
The warmth and fragrance derived from July sun.
I am unable to view the dazzling brightness of landscape
The shadows of lace do not drape the hillsides.

The waters have lost their Tiffany gleam.
Instead it is like molten metal, silver at best.
There is no transparency as the waves lap the shore.
Only bands of iron turning to crash on matted sand.

Red, whites and blues of dress are not noticeable,
Covered by drab olive slickers
To protect from the constant drip of water.
Water, opaque, no more the gems falling from summer skies.

The chill, no warmth in the July air.
A sweater at best, no bikini in evidence.
A vacation filled with windshield wipers.
My, what a summer of grey.

Travel that road of grey.
Take me to a destination of color while
Enjoying this monochromatic journey,
Experiencing that silver palate.

Then warmth felt
The brilliance of friendly smiles
Arms that bring warmth
A home filled with the sunshine of welcome.

Color is again with me!

## A Special Time

It was a beautiful, sunny day.
The Vermont sky was blue and cloudless.
The friends chatty and together.
The old logging road told our path.

It was a joy to be able to walk and see.
It was a time of remembering and yet,
All was new, as we had never been here before.
A walk started, our senses honed, we began.

The swimming pond on the left,
Joder's "Small Michigan Farm" house on the right,
The call from the rooster filled our ears.
Then silence as trees muffled all sound.

The creek with its flat stones rippled below us.
The stones in the road tripped us, annoying until,
The heart-shaped stone was coveted and pocketed!
The broken stone walls peaked around the fern.

I wondered at the fallen trees,
Had they been heard as they crashed to earth?
I breathed in the smell of Christmas
As we were surrounded by pine.

There were buttercups, butterfly weed, Queen Ann's lace,
Daisies, moss and fungi of many hues.
Beautiful dainty flowers, I know not their names.
There in a bountiful bouquet for our eyes.

Our steps faltered as weary we became
And homeward bound were our steps.
Then we were to notice red leaves in our path
Maybe summer was homeward bound also.

We laughed and talked and remembered.
Destinations yet to be walked
Memories to be gathered
All in a Vermont Walk.

Then home to the spring-fed pool.
Clothes to be discarded
Warm flesh to be cooled
The sounds of shivers and splashes.

The sun rose above us.
The hollyhocks nodded to us.
The astilbes of red and pink enjoyed our romp.
Yet the sharing of that walk, this swim, our talk,

Coupled with the beauty of Vermont

Was special!


(For Carol)

### Beautiful Moth

You knocked on our door,
We did not hear you.
Still in a partial cocoon
Legs and arms holding onto the screen
Your body, a spin of threads.
Did you need our help?

Your fluttering caught our eye,
Your wings, your glorious wings:
Six inches of gossamer, pale green,
Sculptured like angel's wings,
Attached to your unfree body.
How can we help?

You are nature at its finest!
Your featherlike antennae quiver.
A Luna Moth is with us.
We admire your uniqueness
With awe and reverence.
We appreciate this rare treat,
We have seen the beauty of nature.

We try to wonder at helping.
Helplessness is upon us,
You seem to understand, so
With extreme wing strength
You fly away.

Never to view you again,
You are now a memory.
Something to reflect upon.
A thought is born:

Moths are not brown, they are beautiful!

Giant Silk Moth (Saturnidae) Luna Moth (Actias luna)
Wingspan: 3-7 _ in. What to look for: spectacularly colored
broad-winged moth, usually with dark out-lined light spots;
featherlike antennae; spiny larva; pupa with cocoon. Habitat:
nearly all land habitats with trees; often near lights.
(Color is pale green.)

*Luna Moth*
*Copyright.... Miriam Adams* 2004

### The Color Green

Find it in a rainbow.
Look for it in a pond.
View it in the racing color of a Jaguar.
Admire it in the flow of emerald chiffon.

Search for it in a box of Binney & Smith Crayons.
Moss green
Blue green
Yellow green
Olive green
Forest green
Pine green
Spring green
Screamin' green
Shamrock green
Sea green
Asparagus
Neon green

That color, green!
Fading as it readies to take a Winter's sleep.
Vacated from your palate as white dominates.
Until a crocus arrives on a dab of wonderful green!
Filling your window after April showers.
Accenting beautiful shades of your garden.

Viewing green can become a joy.
Stand on the edge of a green meadow.
Raise your eyes to the horizon,
And behold the green of Vermont!
The greening of Mt. Abraham,
How many shades?

The ever green of the pines.
The yellow green of early maples.
The green softened by the white of birch.
The promise of harvest in the green of apple orchards.
The northern green of moss.
The cool and refreshing green in a Jack in the Pulpit
Touched by the clear stream,
 Reflecting the power of green, tasting from the bank.

Sit on the bank and feel its greenness.
Run your fingers over the new life emerging.
See the flash of green in the scales of a trout.
Test the green temperature with your toes.
Look up into the blue sky through green fringe.
Spread your Dartmouth green blanket and
Dream awhile, you are on vacation.

As the Green Mountains take on a hue of purple
I know I have traveled outside their greenness.
I look for a rainbow in the drab and clouded sky.
Still looking for a green memory to tuck away,
Then I know that memories will be forever found:

In the word of a poet
In the eye of a photographer
On the brush of an artist
Loomed by the weaver
Forged with love by an artisan
Blown into the glass with determination,
The green of Vermont.

When I return I will find:
An awakening of a life accented with green.
Green so strong I can spell it, **greene**.
Feel the **greene** of cloth and glass.
Admire the **greene** put to canvas.
Read my verse to the **greene** hills,

For the Green Mountains call
And I have been able to answer.

## Stone Walls and Stepping Stones

Look!  Are they not beautiful?
Can you see the texture?
Feel the coldness of the stone?
In these beautiful walls.
These designated soldiers of property.

They stand between acreage.
Denoting ownership,
Visually marking deeds,
Quietly guarding entry,
Steadfastly withstanding the times,

They salute our past.

As I view these walls,
I not only see, but I hear:

The rattle of chains,
The grunt of oxen and mules,
The voices of encouragement,
The scraping of rock upon rock,

And

I smell the sweat of animal and man.

Clearing the fields for planting,
Rocks must be moved,
Rocks to be piled,
Survey and mark the boundary,
Their use now understood,
Their bulk a "monumental" task.

A monument to those who labored.

I take a breath and find "Stepping Stones".
A retreat from the hustle
A place to relax,
A place at the end of a stone wall.

I find today with yesterday's echoes.
A barn filled with bantams.
Roosters and hens hustle to the kitchen door,
Breakfast is being thrown.
Beautiful feathers shine in the sun,
Birds feast at feeders.
Cats laze on the porch.
A German Shepherd stands guard.
Anne smiles.

Her house offers you a welcome.
Its shelves are crammed with books.
Its walls are hung with art and soul.
Its cupboards are full of beautiful crockery.
Crannies are stocked with wonders.
Its kitchen a place to enjoy and talk.

Talk you may,
About everything and anything.
There is knowledge to be tapped,
Knowing to be shared.
Caring abounds.

After filling-up on house cuisine,
Meandering into the garden,
Onto "Stepping Stones",
You wander through gardens.
Trees lovingly planted,
Flowers to greet your eyes
To sweeten your nose.
Paths to hidden turns,
Birdhouses guarding quiet nooks.
A haven in which to rest.

Yes, Anne has fashioned a respite
From flora and stone.
Adding fauna to love
"Stepping Stones" can be found:

Where the road turns,
A road well marked by stone walls.

## Chapter VII
## A Whirlwind of Wandering

My grandson, Tyler, and I flew to Montana to visit our friends, the Greasons, and to spend special time together. **Discovering Montana** was a thank you for a wonderful vacation! **This Place** was written at Canyon Ranch where I found a week of caring and beauty. The fun of **Initial Talk** masks the true meaning of an army base, Fort Rucker, Alabama. It was my first encounter with military and it was overwhelming. I had wandered into the real world, our young men training for combat; Fort Rucker is the Army's helicopter base. Retired Colonel R. W. Bailey helped me to understand the word: duty.

## Discovering Montana

Just a plane ride away
Not such a big deal
Through the twin cities,
Destination:  Bozeman, Montana.

From the edges of Long Island Sound
To the top of Canyon Mountain.
A few days of being with someone special
A time set aside to listen and learn.

Fly fishing, friendships renewed, beautiful vistas.
I guess you must travel far to find purity
Finding it was worth the time spent
Enjoying it, never to be forgotten.

The bed and breakfast located on a downtown street.
The softness of its red brick façade
The woodworking of its staircase
The embellished Victorian décor.

Adventures under the Big Sky:
Getting to know young men
Watching friendships grow
Learning to fly fish.

A welcome so warm
The sharing of knowledge and love of Montana
Beckoning us to partake and enjoy
The days unfolding into our journey.

Shopping for rods, reels, flies and Merrills.
Teenage impatience to don waders and fish!
No time for the quaintness of Bozeman shopping,
A fishing license obtained in the only shop of interest,
The Bozeman Angler.

Tyler was in his element.

I do not think even he was ready for the beauty
A need to catch a fish paramount.
Zane became our guide
To be called, "Fearless Leader".

Tom and Taylor, the elder statesmen.
Barbara Ann our tour guide.
MSU was viewed from the home on the hill
And the beauty of Montana awaited us.

You could almost feel the rawness
Feel the pioneer spirit in mountains never changing
Hear the creak of wagons, the rush of water in sluices
Brought to life on the wooden sidewalks of Virginia City.

The reason for Montana
Found in its strains of ore, forgotten today
Only remembering from this time forth
The beauty of its streams, lakes and mountains.

I will always find humor in the names:
Petterson, Willson, Curtiss, Knaab.
Add one letter more to make a statement.
I think God added just a little more to:

Make Montana, the state.

We fished the Ruby, the Hyalite and viewed the Madison.
Walked the edge of waters under purple mountains
On paths leading to majestic falls
Trees surrounded us with their greenness and aroma.

We practiced the pure outdoor sport, fly fishing.
Rumors of its importance to oneself, never is realized
Until the fly is chosen and the leader sings overhead.
Now understanding, and never yet to catch that fish.

Then, with a setting sun
A darkening of the sky
The mountains calling
One last cast, and bingo:

A fish on the line!

Tyler had caught his fish!.
His smile, a little broader than usual
Telling us of his triumph
He had landed his fish and,

Montana had captured Tyler.

Good-byes were hard to say.
Thank yous very sincere.
Promises to return, so easy.
Memories placed in a book,

Montana and the Greasons,
In the process of remembering
Will be found in the turn of every page
And smiles will reflect beauty and friendship.

Thank you.

Tyler Cabrera fishing the Hyalite.

# This Place

Standing next to a saguaro cactus
I note its majesty and thorns.
It offers its trunk to house Arizona birds,
Almost embracing their nester's choice.
I feel the presence of yesterday in their fruit.
Brown hands attached to long sticks harvesting
These ripe blossoms as they turned to bright red.
Vats were fired, making the heat intense.
Stirring produced the staple, cactus jelly.

The chefs of chiefs are no more.
The fires are cold, the primitive recipe forgotten.
Let not these ancestors be forgotten.
Allow me to caress that brown skin,
Plait that black hair,
Watch Indian campfires alight with ritual,
I must stand on this land
Please, touch me with the spirit living in these mountains.

Through eyes of black now mine of blue,
See these mountains and understand their strength.
Raise eyes above the peaks to the azure ceiling.
Sky traveled by billowing white clouds
Sky sparkling with millions of stars
Sky angry with monsoon lightening and thunder
Catch our imagination as they scream their dominance.
Mountains and sky surround **This Place** with their difference.

**This Place** is of sand and stone,
Mesquite, eucalyptus and cactus.
Frogs the color of that sand
Call out in voices the color of deep purple.
There are rabbits who recline like pampered cats,
Doves who coo, "Good Morning",
Rattlers who shake, rattle and move (hopefully)
And coyotes whose howls are heard only by the moon.

Yes, they are all part of **This Place**.

I amble down paths well designed to confuse,
As witnessed by the abundance of arrows.
Doors to buildings of learning and sleeping
Whose color and architecture blend with the earth
Are my final destination, on any given hour.
High winds, rain and darkened sky,
Feeling like Dorothy I call for Auntie Em.
With a laugh and no fear, I find my way home.

At each turn of the path I was awarded with a smile.
Behind each door I found a friend.
Each gym housed a caring professional.
Every office crammed full of knowledge to share.
Facing each class, a trained ambassador.
Hands and tables offered a warm touch.
Comfort at allowing control to shift,
A feeling of security and love abound.

All a part of **This Place**.
Collected here, in this place,
Likened to gold settling to the bottom of a prospector's tin.
Yes, pure gold of different shapes and weights,
Per ounce, a veritable treasure.
A strike here in these beautiful mountains.
A lode so pure it dazzles
I am sharing the wealth, how grand!

Physically I have sweated and stretched.
Mentally I have sweated tears and stretched.
Yesterday became no more
Today became intense
Tomorrow became a possibility.
Those gathered here at *Canyon Ranch* have
Clearly marked my path,
Steadied my gait.
They wish me never to fall again.

Yes, all in **This Place**.


Written at Canyon Ranch, Tucson, Arizona

63

### Initial Talk

More than ABC.
Order of utmost importance.
When heard, information aplenty,
Unless,

Initials are the carriers of information!
Military at its best,
Civilian at its most unawareness,
Conversation flows, only "Yes, Sirs" understand.

Caught a few, such as ID.
Knew that one: Identification.
I'm in the Army now!
Or, so I thought.

Going to the NCO Club.
Dressing in BDU's.
Parking in CSM's spot.
A member of the TROA.
Shopping at the PX.

In the sky, a HUEY.
Introduced to an IP
Flying a H58.
Grab a letter, everyone else is.

There's a tank.
Wrong, it's an APC.
Wow, look a helicopter.
No, it's a H64 with a FLIR.

So, I begin to think alphabet.
Join in, the water's fine,
Or is that H2o?
Have to learn to survive
If not, I'll need R & R.

"He was my Executive Officer."
"Oh, your EO?"
"No, my XO."
Well, I tried!

You can't just visit alphabet land.
You must drive through its gates with Military ID.
You must live on the field.
Fly in its skies.
Frolic with its personnel.
Understand the need for quick identity.
Solve problems that mean life or death to others.
Work as a team, two-man or battalion.
Feel the intensity of the fabric.
Respect a definite way of life.
Salute years of service.
Admire dedication.
Be patriotic beyond call

And

Be able to converse in **Initial Talk**.

To:  RW from HNC

## Chapter VIII
## A Special Place to Enjoy

Wanderings took me down a road of service. It is a time of celebration when you are again able to give of yourself. The reward of adding friendship and caring into your life is healing. You begin when others enjoy who you are and what you have to offer.

I was able to meet and be part of a program at the Samaritan House For Boys in Stuart, Florida. Dr. Bob Bedingfield understood my need to contribute and was very supportive of my role as a poet. He suggested teaching this class and, with his help, submitted a teaching outline to the board. It was wonderful, yet scary. Could I handle a class in poetry for young boys? Well, I did and found joy in the process. **My Class** and **Cookies and Milk** proved you can find reciprocal need if you just share yourself. Meandering at its best!

## My Class

*George* of the sweet face.
*Wide-eyed, glasses round,*
*Stature small, presence felt.*
  *So young, so vulnerable.*

*Jason* with his shoulders square.
*Aware and wary*
*This leader of the class*
*May fear not be the reason for love*
  *Love of his mates.*

*Roy*, The Worrier.
*Quiet, always viewing, yet touchable.*
*Unable to open as a new bud should,*
*Yet perishable when in full bloom.*
  *Dark even in youth*

*Donald*, the mind direct to:
*The world calling to him.*
*His knowledge of the habitat*
*From the sun to the sky to turtles.*
  *His poetry fills the pages.*

*David*, grown, yet so young.
*Wanting to speak, unable to be still.*
*Vulnerable as a growing puppy*
*To please, yet to disrupt.*
  *May success sweeten his life.*

My **Paul**.  *Always out of his seat*
*Glue may do, but "please sit" works.*
*Pictures rather than words.*
*Always viewing the others.*
  *A need to be accepted.*

*Carl* watches and asks.
*Help with the simplest rhymes.*
*No focus, yet interest is there.*
*Hopefully help will be on its way.*
  *Fill him with confidence*

*Jake*, quiet, round face, gray eyed.
*He fills his seat with his body*
*His mind fills the room,*
*Yet, he writes not.  I wonder.*
  *Please give him a voice.*

*Devan* with hand up and mind off.
*The pencil has no lead, just a need.*
*A need to be part of this class*
*His answer:  an email address!*
  *If only he would just write.*

### This is "My Class"

67

## Cookies and Milk

When I was young it was:

Time out from studies,
A treat on the way!
A rest for the brain,
Cookies and milk time!

Relax,
Sugar and cow juice on the menu.
Nothing better than cookies,
Nothing healthier than milk.

But,

Together on a tray
They spell: SPECIAL!
For student and teacher
Cookie Time awaits.

Now that I am older:

Cookies are a way of reaching out.
I make cookies for all occasions,
Christmas, Easter, Birthday,
My way of saying "Thank You"

For:

A wonderful family day.
A loving moment.
A gesture of friendship.
A memorable event.
A shared experience.

*Or:*

*To chase away the blues.*
*To bring on a smile.*
*To receive a hug.*

*Or:*

*Just because,*
*Because I love my Chocolate Chip Cookies!!*

*Cookies and milk are special.*
*They represent feelings.*
*Feelings shared,*
*Feelings baked between the morsels.*

*A cookie melts in your mouth.*
*A cookie tastes like all good things:*

*Wonderful!*

*A cookie sums up your day:*

*Successful!*

*A toast to every cookie ever eaten.*
*A double toast to every cookie still to be dunked.*
*So, clink that cookie against the glass,*
*Close your eyes and enjoy!!*

*We'll talk about vegetables tomorrow,*

*Maybe.*

# Chapter IX
## Meeting and Saying Goodbye

Can you remember all the different times people have come into your life when you needed them?

Stuart Hemingway was one of those people. At my husband's memorial mass the pianist did not arrive and Stuart graciously came to the rescue. He added our special musical requests to this important day. Meeting this blind pianist for the first time and then spending time with him as he tried to teach me the piano, offered me the opportunity for our friendship. When a stroke took away Stuart's playing ability, our community grieved for him. A party was held so that we could all remind Stuart how important he was to all of us. My granddaughter, Brooke, and I played "Heart and Soul" and I wrote **Hemidemisemiquaver**.

Rider University was fortunate having for its president, J. Barton Luedeke. He welcomed me and encouraged me to return to the Lawrenceville campus. His retirement gave me the opportunity to send kudos and a bit of fun in his direction with **A Fond Farewell**.

He has always there for me, and for everyone in Old Greenwich. Tom Stiers is the most compassionate man I have ever met. I needed him and he was there for me. On his retirement (all my dear friends were moving on) I contributed **The Caring Thomas** to his memory book.

*A special place to list special people!*

## A Hemidemisemiquaver

Not a whole note.
One/sixteenth of a crotchet.
One/half of a demisemiquaver.
You are a hemidemisemiquaver.
A 64th note,
Lovingly, that's how Stu appears to me.

Not tall in stature,
Just big of heart.
A whole note beats,
To the rhythm of drums.
To the understanding of jazz.
To the sound of piano
To the love of music.
To the talent of living
To the gift of befriending
To the openness of self:

Only a 64th left for himself:
He's a true Hemidemisemiquaver

In three-quarter time he shares his knowledge.
His tempo, adagio, when explaining the lesson.
Allegretto showing how it is accomplished.
Prestissimo with his feel for the music.
I know he is Italian, that talent!

His talent an unbelievable joy, but
His vision is what has always amazed me.
That vision into one's ability, or non ability.
The visions of your needs, musical or other.
His ability to see you as a friend, and care.
If we all could have just a fraction of his insight.
We would rejoice.

Those lessons:
His listening ear, hearing my wrong choice.
Never cringing, always gracious.
His helping hand, showing how.
His voice on tape, reminding how.
My trying to learn, not able to focus, yet
I loved my hour in the house on Summit.

A symphony is a work with movements.
The first movement usually
Sets the mood.
The second movement is often complex
Appears to slow down.
The third movement becomes faster
In reality, shorter.
The fourth movement is a wrap up,
It must be upbeat!!
Stuart Hemingway, you are a symphony!

Life is your stage,
My hemidemisemiquaver.
Your friends will always be your back-up group.
You are a class act,
One that we applaud every day!

# A Fond Farewell

He doesn't look like Franklin F. Moore,
Not even J. Goodner Gill.
He doesn't act like FFM,
More like JGG.
But, the truth be known,
He is just himself.

His sly smile,
The slight tilt of the head,
Direct eye contact, with a twinkle,
(As though we share a secret),
Forthright and friendly, a special man.

Behind the outward, easy-going demeanor
There is much to know.

His intense intellect.
His ability to communicate,
His knowledge of the moment's inquiry,
His compassion,
His need to listen,
His desire to care,
His insight into financial spending,
His far-sighted goals,
His success in reaching those goals,
His genuine interest in his work,
His awareness of your smile, or absence of one,
His respect for Rider, faculty and students,
His love for his family.

His name may take you a while to learn.
His schedule will always have room for you.
His notes will be on the mark.
His hand-written comments are funny and thoughtful.

Who could this be?

Ludeke or is that Luedeke?

No matter how you spell it,
How you pronounce it,
He will answer with that smile,
A welcoming handshake or hug.

You have just met:

A gentleman:  J. Barton Luedeke.

p.s. Good luck, not good bye.

## The Caring Thomas

It was a time of deep grief.
It was a time of not knowing.
It was a time of confusion.
It was a time of needing counsel.
Where to turn?
I am alone, I need help.
I need to reach out.
Who will listen?

From our first meeting,
A marriage.
To years of smiles and hellos.
"How are the grandchildren?"
Often asked.
Always interested,
Never hurried enough not to care.
Maybe he would help.
I had an answer, Tom Stiers.

In the hospital,
It was Tom who wondered at my presence.
A touch, a question, an embrace.
I entered Jim's room with a smile.
I was able to take a deep breath.
A miracle of another's compassion.

Then, death.

One year was over,
Tom joined with us at the cemetery.
Breakfast was next,
He made time for us.
Always there to administer when needed.
He made God's presence felt.

*Now I must face life, alone.*
*I do not know how.*
*I am making mistakes.*
*Can I call Tom?*
*I reached for the phone,*
*He was there for me.*

*The counseling quieted me.*
*His listening quelled my frantic ways.*
*Most unbelievable was the understanding,*
*The nonjudgmental reasoning.*
*Tom's worldly, yet church-like counsel.*
*"You must go on",*
*GAVE ME HOPE.*

*The gift of Hope.*
*Given to me by such a dedicated minister,*
*In such a gracious manner,*
*Gleaning no promises for tomorrow,*
*Just emphatically stressing: happiness today,*
*Be yourself; enjoy yourself and your family,*
*Write, create and love.*

*Dear Tom, special is the right word!*
*You opened the door of contentment in religion,*
*You enable me to share my work,*
*You gave me confidence to write,*
*You would be there when I needed you to listen.*
*You took time to care.*

*Thank you.*

# *Chapter X*
## *Wandering and Remembering*

As I rest from my recent wanderings I remember. It is always a useful tool to keep you on the right path to remember where you have been before you continue. I was reminded of that by the comedian, Billy Crystal. When asked about his success he related the following: As a young boy he would always do a routine while brushing his teeth, using the brush as his microphone. He keeps a toothbrush in his pocket because "you should always remember where you came from".

**I Use' Ta Ride The Bus** is a poem that reminds me who I am. Yes, I did ride a bus and I know I can do it again if need be and not be fearful. Remembering the importance of a penny will keep your value system intact. **I Found A Penny** does just that as I remember the family that honed these values. **Your Phone Number** is a link to the past, but since my sister has kept that same number in Pennsylvania, I can always call home as I meander. It does not cost a penny or even time, as I travel with **A Mother's Gift**. During a truly remarkable memorial service for a wonderful and gallant lady, Ginny Tierney, her son thanked his mother for giving him a gift of faith.

Yes, you should always remember where you have been. It will enable you to go forward.

## I Use' Ta Ride the Bus

Sitting in my Jag
Waiting at the light
Humming along to Sinatra
Life is pretty damn good.

Thinking of what next,
Needing a project,
Wanting a focus.
What's next?

Then the public bus turns the corner.

I see people looking out,
I look in at the passengers and
Memories flooded into my window,
I was 16 again, riding the bus.

The bus stopped to pick up.

I am the one standing on the corner.
I pay my dime and take a seat.
I say hello to those I know.
I watch for my stop.

I ring the bell and the back door opens.

The years fly by.
The streets have different names.
The mode of travel more individualized.
But I am the same, though a little older.

The need for a bus is no more.

But,

If ever I need to travel the streets
I know I will be able to wait at a stop,
Climb aboard with the others,
Pay my fare and say hello

Because: **I use' ta ride the bus.**

### I Found A Penny!

It sat on the sidewalk, head up,
Right where those who pass could see.
It was bright and coppery
But it was "only a penny".

As I bent to retrieve my treasure
I remembered hundreds of befores.
Always into my pocket
Thinking how lucky I was.

Songs like: "Pennies From Heaven"
Ran through my mind onto my lips.
My walk took on a skip mode.
And I felt a little richer.

Is picking up a penny not chic?
Has its worth diminished?
As a child I knew not chic
And it bought a precious piece of candy.

I wonder at the value of a penny,
I wonder at the values of a generation
I ponder on what I know and remember
I question my questions and try to understand.

Generation after generation after generation
And then another, two behind, one then, one now.
The world spins and time moves us forward
Age become reality and remembering a must.

My grandparents lived an austere life.
Filled with work, in and out of the home.
Labor-hard, canning-hard, garden-hard,
A day whose hours numbered many without sleep.

Those hands, callused, lovingly caressing me.
They taught me to prune perennials
They showed me the fruit of a garden.
They cooked and fed my body and soul.

And, they always picked up a penny.

My Mother and Father were depression children.
Their creed: "Every penny counts".
Leftovers found their way into omelets and soups.
We questioned their frugality often.

We picked four leaf clovers and made violet chains.
Vacations were sparse and wardrobes homemade.
Although no canning or gardening, this generation,
Hard work remained, saving was for college tuitions.

Counting every penny found and banked!

Role models leave their mark on our lives
Negative as well as positive.
You value and revalue and choose
Your pocket jingles with pennies.

You spend and twirl with a life of freedom.
Freedom of mind and a future coppery bright.
A new house, a new car and babies to love.
No leftovers in my soup!

But I still smile as I approach a lost penny!

My children have gone off to college.
Our pennies spent have enabled them to grow.
Our hard work at home and away made it possible,
Our role models deserve all the credit.

Today I await their visit from afar.
Grandchildren for me to love and caress.
Pennies have purchased gifts under a sparkling tree
But one gift, my wish, lights the star atop:

Find many shiny pennies, please, dear ones,
Take the time to stop and pick them up!

## Your Phone Number

When did you first hear the ring?
Were you crawling, caught your attention?
It was black and not too attractive,
When did it become so important?

Did you receive a "No"
When you tottered to examine?
Did it cause you concern
When your parent opted for it rather than you?

Years were entwined with its existence.
Very different interactions, some good, some not so.
Then the teen years.
And a friend made for life!

The bridge to the outside when curfew hit.
Your number, BLackburn 2-0795, wow!
Anytime you needed a friend, just dial,
Share a secret, learn the facts, accessible, just dial.

The ring was two short,
A long ring, another on the party line.
Listen, is it for you, yes,
So cuddle up and talk.

Until that party on the line
Tries to use the phone, oops,
Have I been on for one hour?
Sorry, your turn, good bye.

So it went for the growing-up years.
A lifeline when you were away at school.
Comforting as a new parent,
"What do I do, the fever is 104 degrees?"

Help was always at, now, 252-0795.
Mom and Dad were home for me and my woes.
No answering machine, just love.
I would never cut the phone cord.

Never a click before, "I love you".
Years became decades, connected still.
Talking became louder, "What?" more often.
Touching, reaching out, family always.

I wonder how many times I dialed,
215-252-0795 now 610-252-0795?
A million or more times.
May I please have another million!

No. For time passes and things change,
Not 252-0795, but those who answer.
Or, those who can never answer again.
For one loved one is gone.

So, when I dial that special number
The one that was mine as a child,
The one that helped me through puberty,
The one that answered my cry for help,

I still get a ring,
A slanted, hellllooo,
My Father's greeting, so him.
I ask, "How long will I get the ring to answer?"

When will that cord of communication be gone.
At 86 his hellloooo is softer,
"Who is this?' is often asked and
I answer, "Your daughter."

My inquiries are of his health,
I am not looking for help, just offering it.
Memories of the room in which the phone is kept
Fill the time until the ring is heard and answered

I know that we must grow old.
I know we must accept time passing.
I know we must ready ourselves for tomorrow.
And, I really do know that someday,

610-252-0795 will no longer belong to me.

## A Mother's Gift

*I oft times wonder where strength is found.*
*During good times as well as bad*
*Strength to go alone among others*
*To walk with dignity and belief.*

*Today, another Christmas, dawned.*
*Alone and yet not forgotten I awoke.*
*The reaching out and touching, so needed.*
*As I sat surrounded by God's love, how, why?*

*Because of a Mother's love.*
*Her love of me and of God.*
*She insisted, much to my resistance,*
*To learn, to feel and to believe.*

*Years have passed and so has She,*
*Leaving behind her love of me and God.*
*I have never questioned Her love,*
*I have sometimes questioned God's love.*

*Alone today in my grief,*
*My Mother's gift of love*
*Reached out to me, in God's hands*
*And placed within my heart a quietness.*

*A quietness and peacefulness now attained.*
*Tomorrow will not change, She is not here,*
*My Father is with her, my Husband has died,*
*Yet, today the loneliness has quieted.*

*Tomorrow will dawn, bringing rain or sun.*
*And I will awaken to another day.*
*A thankfulness will fill me enough to force a smile.*
*I shall walk with joy and respect because of*

*The gift of a Mother's love:  Her faith.*

*Thank you, Mommy.*

# Chapter XI
## Tributes

There are always the good memories. Even when you look inside to see who you are, where you have been and where you are going, the extent of those moral and social boundaries that are you, you still have the feeling that you are special and different. That is what enables you to go forth. A time to stop the tears and use that mind that remembers even the smallest detail to bring you contentment with yourself and your world.

My Father became ill and I went home. It was a bittersweet time. To see this strong, handsome man, who worked so hard to provide for us, becoming frail was heart breaking. It was just the two of us, father and daughter, caring for each other. He talked about his love for my Mother and how he missed her (she has been gone two years). This time was spent doing everyday chores and not thinking of tomorrow. When that tomorrow came I wrote **His Hands II** (**His Hands** is found in *My Journey, The Loss Of A Loved One)* to be read as his eulogy.

You are often called to remember the past, especially when the past will equate to more time then is left to speculate. Frank (Conky) Solana was best man at our wedding and Jim's classmate, so when their 50th class reunion from White Plains High School was planned I was asked to participate. For the memorial service held in their auditorium I wrote **Sleeping Tigers**. I remembered all that Jim had shared with me over the years and his love of WPHS found its way into this poem. Causing others to remember and relate was rewarding.

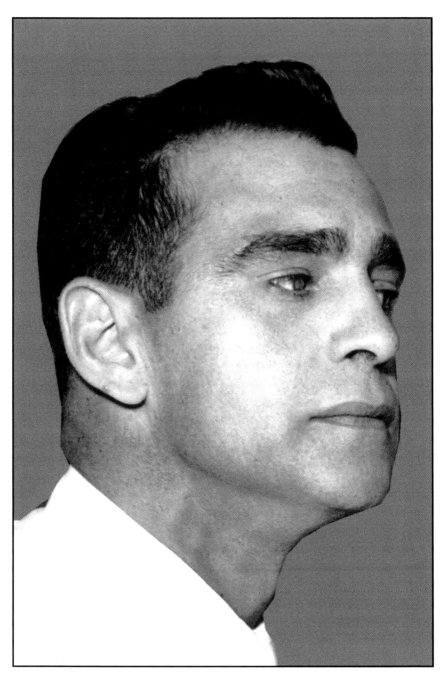

*My Father, Anthony (Pete) Napoli 1956*

## His Hands II

A year has gone
The hospital stay still a reality
Yet, time has not stood still
Tomorrow is here, right now.

His hands have grown older.
They are never still.
Stillness comes to mind with dread
Yet, movement is an agitation.

I wonder if movement is a need?
Does the activity without cause peace within?
Not a shaky movement,
A movement with intense productivity.

The rustle of a held piece of paper.
The strumming on a table top.
The feeling of fabric.
The use of fingers in lieu of utensils.
The constant exercise of stretching and relaxing.
The straightening of a napkin.
The viewing of every nail and cuticle.
The touching of one's face.

No more the need to fondle.
No more the need to slice and prepare.
No more the use of strength during a day.
Even the clicker is silent.

The pain of observation
The realization of aging
The acknowledging of what is to come
Please, dear hands, continue to be.

*I care not if the strumming agitates,*
*I worry not if the rustling disturbs,*
*I overlook the sameness in motion,*
*I ask just one thing:*

*Dear hands, continue to be.*
*Continue in my life.*
*Let me feel their warmth.*
*Allow me to reach for familiar fingers.*

*For I belong holding that which is mine,*
*That which is part of me,*
*The memories and love.*
*Let them hold my hands,*

*As my children will someday hold mine,*

*With respect and joy of what has been.*

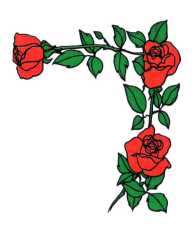

*The right time to write a little about your parents.*

## Sleeping Tigers

Just cubs,
Not full grown, yet
Ready to learn.
Their lair:
The school on the Highlands.

It took "the pride" three years.
They experienced the pain of youth
While soaking up knowledge.
The bells signaled classes to change,
The whistle signaled games ending,
The years quickly passed.

Refrains of your alma mater,
The Orange And The Black,
Graduation and good-byes.
Signing the Oracle, cats galore.
New adventures and hellos.
No time to look back,
Todays held so much excitement,
As the tigers crouched, ready to spring.

Their roars heard in many arenas.
Their prints on many documents.
Time passes,
And reluctantly
The roars quiet.

Now 50 years have passed.
The cubs have come home again.
Grown and anxious to relive that youth,
They gather to celebrate.

Celebrate that "pride" of the Highlands.
Celebrate successes and family.
Celebrate the joy of friendship.
Celebrate this minute. . . . . .Now,

Please, reflect on those sleeping tigers:
Your classmates whose roars are no longer heard.
Sing about the lilies slender,
Reach into your memory bank and remember,
Remember them as cubs,
Embrace them as tigers,

Rejoice at their being here with you today, In spirit:

The Spirit of the White Plains High School Class of 1953

# Chapter XII
## Reaching Out

The response to **Sleeping Tigers** was rewarding. Many expressed the comfort they found from my words as they remembered their classmates and their time in high school. I felt honored to be part of the reunion.

I had written two pieces that dealt with the need not only to comfort, but to comfort with understanding. The issue being addressed was the ability to comfort when you have not experienced grief or other painful situations. Can you really understand? Can you offer the right words of comfort? These pieces fit into the book and within that poetry there was an answer. It was the understanding that I would never truly know the pain of some of the subjects that affect another's life, but could always be compassionate. My tears come easily when I feel another's pain, but the need to understand and comfort in a positive way is so important.

As you read **Understanding** and **To Comfort, A Time Arrived**, look for the relationship between a person's understanding of a situation and a person's ability to offer meaningful comfort. At times the pieces reflect the same thoughts, just as comforting can be accomplished without a full understanding but must be coupled with compassion.

## Understanding

Can you,

If you have not walked,
Walked in the shoes of another?

Have you known:
The pain of losing a child,
The agony of watching a loved one die,
The helplessness as parents age,
The frustration of an invalid,
The desperation of no new medical news,
The aches of years upon the bone and muscle?

Can you?  Do you?

Not when you console with these words:
Time will heal,
Old age is a state of mind,
They have led a good life,
Medical research is searching for a cure,
Call me if you need me.

No true understanding,
Clichés, because you do not know.
Honest concern, not true understanding.
Yes?  No?  Just step back, question.

Do you truly understand the feelings of:
An illiterate,
A member of a dysfunctional family,
A person born with a birth defect?

What about:
Poverty,
Hunger,
Sexual abuse,
Filth,
Death,
Loneliness,
All personal hells as an adult.
Unfathomable as a child.

Can you feel the probability,
Does it cause sightlessness?
Don't close your eyes, look around.
It is next door, a bus ride away,
But, it is here.

I know you shake your head.
You cannot truly understand.
You have not walked in their shoes,
Or walked without shoes,
I understand that you do not know.

But,

Try compassion, try helping,
Full understanding is not an option,
Reaching out is, try,
It will enrich your life,
You will make a difference.

Full understanding will not come
Until that day when the shoes fit
And, unfortunately, you will then,

Understand completely.

## To Comfort, A Time Arrived

I may find a need to understand
A need to comfort
Comforting, a part of me
As necessary as breathing.

Who will comfort?
Who knows how to comfort?
Can anyone comfort?
Is comforting acceptable?

Can I comfort those who have lost a child?
Can I understand the unhappiness of divorce?
Within my reach can I successfully touch the dying?
Am I able to feel the despair of the crippled?
Is my advice to a sibling who is not mine relevant?
When another's aging parent calls for help, can I answer?
I think not.

For, do I not cringe at comfort offered by those who:
Have not lost a spouse.
For, they do not understand completely
My soul and heart are amiss, and they do not know.

I want to be comforted by the wounded comforter.
The words I want to hear must reach my soul.
The hands that hold mine
Must have held hands that are no longer here.

Understand my pain and my loss,
Though mine alone, must be understood.
You cannot comfort successfully unless you know,
Unless it is the same comfort you yearn to receive.

Listen to those who reach out.
Advise not, just listen and care.
Your turn to be a wounded comforter may come,
Until then, just listen and care.

# Chapter XIII
## A Time to Remember

When the sun set on September 11, 2001 the world had changed. I had wandered into a surreal happening. Until I located my New York-working son, Joe, I was suspended by fear, the same fear that many were to realize. With tears flowing I penned: **The Day The New York Skyline Changed**. My wandering ceased at this time. I was glued to the television, hardly believing what I saw.

Two months later I was asked to read this poem at an alumni gathering for Rider University in Rye, New York. At the reception a beautiful Irish face introduced himself as a New York firefighter stationed at Lincoln Center and a Rider grad. Mr. Tim Callaghan expressed his pride in being a firefighter and a Rider alumni. His heartfelt thank you made the moment special. The emotion of the minute has been tucked into a special place and my poem was posted in the fire station.

Wanderings became my focus the winter of 2005. Getting it ready for publication was joyful. At the chapel in the community where I live in Florida there was an exhibit of the work of a very talented photographer, Michael McNamara. I was so excited, I found a companion to my 9.11 poem. It was entitled "Sunrise" and dated 9.12. As I was viewing the skyline from Connecticut, Mike captured for all times that skyline from New Jersey. As sad as we will always feel, the birds in flight bring life into the framed negative. This picture appears in the book within that frame, emphasizing the necessity of our never forgetting.

*Mike McNamara (Photographer)   Sunrise 9.12*

### The Day The New York Skyline Changed

The date:  9.11.01
Call 911, call for help
But from the 100th floor?
Can this be real?

Cell phones with mayday tones
Voices knowing they will never be heard again.
Anger and hatred touching our lives
Filling our homes with disbelief and grief.

Why? When? How?, surreal at best.
But before our eyes, the truth.
Destruction beyond our imagination
Loss of loved ones, never again to hold.

This Tuesday in September
Another Sunday in December remembered.
How do we react as a country?
How do we manage as an individual?

My eyes have seen
My ears have heard
But my heart cannot comprehend
I can only reach out with my mind.

Imagine the dedication of a fireman
Climbing against the throng
To do what he had been trained to do.
Climbing to his death!

I am unable to imagine the fear
Unable to comprehend reactions
As the floors gave way
As today ended, today.

Only reaction,
Only disbelief,
Only the knowing it to be real.
Only the feeling of loss.

No anger, not yet.
Sadness and a quiet atmosphere as
I viewed the N. Y. skyline, this a.m.
From the shores of Long Island Sound.

No "Good Morning" to those gathered.
Remorse frozen on unsmiling faces.
The feeling of complete shock envelops us,
As does the quiet of the planeless sky.

Time is standing still.
The heartbeat of New York silenced.
Its people touch and administer
As billowing smoke becomes part of:

The New Skyline of New York City.

Never to disappear

# Chapter XIV
## Wandering and Sharing

**Just Imagine** was written months after the tragedy of 9.11. Every day news reached out to me about the pain and suffering. I remembered another time that still haunts me. The memories of movie theatre screens bringing to me the faces of the Jewish people being evacuated from concentration camps, their eyes and bodies were again part of my life. At the time I prayed for them and over the years I often wondered what happened to them. The poem was my way of trying to realize another's pain.

I talked a lot about **Just Imagine** and my need to place it in my book. I could not just piece it in, I needed some personal understanding. How? In 2004 I found it! Having brunch with a friend from Brazil, Vicky Block, I told her that 9.11 has triggered my memories of Nazi oppression and thus the piece. I told her its contents and she looked at me with tears in her eyes. That poem was about her Grandmother. Her story:

Clara Schnitzer was fixing apple strudel for dinner when the OSS broke through the door and demanded that she and her older daughter, Erika, come with them to clean an office building in Berlin. Hitler's staff was arriving the next day. They worked all night and when they were ready to leave he grabbed Erika and said she was to stay. Clara pleaded with the officer to spare her daughter. She pressed upon him the family's German heritage and four generations of service to Germany. He reluctantly allowed them to leave. The very next day the family fled to Brazil. Portuguese became their language, they never spoke German again, Clara never baked another apple strudel.

I was fortunate to be sent a picture of Erika Schnitzer Block; it was the thread I needed to complete my thoughts and it gave my poem life!

Will there ever be peace in the world? Can mutual respect be present even though we differ in so many respects? When I wrote **My Piece I Give You** it filled a need to offer myself, a piece of myself in the form of acceptance. I promised myself I would never allow even the smallest bit of prejudice into my home.

*Erika Schnitzer Block  2004*

### Just Imagine

The end of a day.
The sun is streaming through the window
Comfort is found in its warmth.
The supper is simmering.
Stew, accompanied by apple strudel,
Wine from the Rhine Valley,
A family favorite.
Find one more piece to your puzzle,
Then to set the table.
But, you speak German.

The children smiled when asked,
"How was your day?"
Your husband will arrive any minute,
"How was your day?",
He will ask the same.
"I had a wonderful day"
Will be your response,
In German.

You hum along as you listen to music.
A Strauss waltz, your choice,
Mozart, your husband's,
Swing is the kids' favorite,
Any words, sung in German.

You move from the puzzle,
Tell the children to wash for supper,
Let the dog out,
Feed the cat,
Reach for the china,
It is German.

A sound catches your ear,
Could he be coming up the walk?
Your smile tells of love.
You turn and the door crashes open.
Men invade your home.
The welcoming mezuzah is torn down.
Your heart stops beating.
Your children appear
You run to protect them with your body.
You try to protect them with words,
Words that are German.

Your world stops.
Your very essence flows from you.
The soul escapes as you fall.
Your eyes cannot see.
Your mind will not function.
Your plea is universal.
The root, German.

Can we imagine?
Imagine is a choice.
Reality is one we do not imagine.
Cannot imagine at our door.
The sound of breaking glass
Will not be heard in our imagining.
It is too painful.

No, we cannot imagine,
For imagining is too painful.

## My Piece I Give You

What an interesting word, peace.
Say peace, could be piece.
Sound the same, different meaning?
In some ways yes,
In other ways no.
My peace I give you,
A piece of me to you.

Can I reach out with only a word
And not an accompanying gesture?
Must this peace I offer you be just vocal,
Cannot it identify also a touch, a connection?
Your eyes must meet mine.
Blue or brown reflect a sameness.
No right or wrong, just brotherhood.

Then why, oh why, is it so difficult?
I offer you peace, not a piece
Of me, of mine, of sharing.
Do you in return offer me peace?
Shalom,
But peace, not a piece.

Of my heart, a piece to understand.
Of my bread, a piece to feed.
Of my land, a piece to harvest.
Of my house, a piece to rest.
Of my book, a piece to read.
Of my love, a piece to accept.

For though different we are

We can find peace,

If we offer a piece of ourselves.

# Chapter XV
## Sharing my Joy

One of the happiest times is when I can be part of the lives of my grandchildren. There are games of football, lacrosse, field hockey and soccer. I enjoy the birthday parties, Sunday family dinners and the greetings as we pass each other in Old Greenwich, Connecticut. I proudly attend concerts, plays, award banquets and graduations. They are good students, amazing on horseback, talented artists, beautiful cheerleaders, fantastic athletes, photographers and poets. **All Me** by Joseph Charles Cabrera (JAKE), age 9, is really who Jake is and he understands himself! Brooke Cabrera, age 12, took time to honor **A Sunset**, so I accompanied her piece with a photograph taken by her brother, Jim Cabrera (age 19), *Footprints Into The Sunset*, taken in Costa Rica. They thrill me.

Even though I must wander, for this is who I am, I want to be part of the lives that my husband and I nurtured over the years. It is comforting to know that we are still bonded together with mutual love and respect and that my sons and daughters-in-law are continuing in that tradition.

Sending one hundred, yes, 100, cards celebrated my birthday. The message and picture marked the beginning of my 69th year, Hear! Hear! It was my way of touching all those who have shared my family. The years from when *My Journey* ended until *Wanderings* are marked with joy, sorrow and love. My need to survive could be found in the envelope.

**Yellow Roses** tells of my desire to be whole again, to be understood, to stand alone. When a yellow rose is extended it may be in the form of a hug, or whatever someone may offer. I chose a yellow rose as a symbol of happiness offered to me because my son, Jim, would often bring me a single yellow rose picked (from a neighbor's bush I am sure) on his way home from grade school. It was a precious time.

### All Me
#### by
#### Jake Cabrera

There is something I can't live without,
That thing is candy without a doubt.

I like football, I am rough and tough,
But my friends think I am crazy and stuff.

I am full of energy.  If you meet me you will know.
It is hard to catch me, I am always on the go.

Football, basketball, lacrosse,
Yep, I play them all.
Come and play with me, you will have a ball.

I have a lot of family and we're tight,
Don't worry, they won't and don't bite.

I have a lot of friends, they're cool,
I met quite a few here at school.

I like my poem, some people do,
I really hope that you do TOO!!

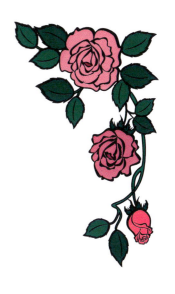

*Write about a child you love.*

*Footprints Into The Sunset ... Costa Rica 2003*
*... James S. Cabrera*

### Sunsets
#### by
#### Brooke C. Cabrera

Sunsets are so beautiful.

As they light up the sky,

They can even change colors,

You could almost die.


Sunsets are so beautiful,

Cooling, calming, captivation,

They are tranquil too,

I think they are romantic,

Don't you?


Sunsets are so beautiful,

Sometimes they set slow,

Sometimes they go fast,

I don't know about you,

But I hope this moment will last.

3·10·04

Another of my natal anniversaries has passed,
And time marches on, relentlessly.
But in my advancing youth, I am constantly aware of the joy
And love and importance of family.
I am truly blessed.
May you sense the happiness I feel for those in the photo,
And know that I value the special friendship and
Experiences we have shared over the years.

**Love on my birthday and everyday,**

*Helen*

*My Birthday Card*

## Yellow Roses

Birthday, it came, it left,
What is the difference?
Does it taint tomorrow,
Change the venue,
Alter the course,
Remind me of yesterday?
It came, it left.

Today is the only day,
Tomorrow another,
Yesterday, the first in a trilogy.
Played to my music,
To the beat of my heart,
To the lyrics of my soul,
This is my song.

I sing alone, sometimes off key.
Never will a duet be heard.
It is too late on the staff,
Not enough room
Words must fit the already set notes.
Energy cannot be generated to change,
I stand alone.

Sharing my space, my thoughts,
Who is listening, who understands?
Why does it matter who cares?
I must listen and care,
Swaying to the beat, I continue.
Hold me in your arms.
My song is singular, my need:

Yellow Roses.

## Chapter XVI
## Time for Tea

Returning to my home in the North, my need for yellow roses is great. The house reminds me of what I have lost. Before unpacking those closet clothes and all the new additions, I wrote **Returning Home**. Hugging myself, knowing that the sun will shine into my yellow bedroom in the morning, I wander to the breakfast table adorned with a bouquet of yellow roses. Now, for a cup of tea.

*On this page, your Yellow Rose request.*

## Returning Home

Open the door,
Feel the yesterdays greet you,
Reach for the warmth of belonging,
Wait for the anxiety to subside,
Anticipate the respite called home.

See the welcoming flowers
Arranged with love and caring.
The balloon bobbing in the wind:
Welcome Home!
Your spring garden awaits your perusal.
Your trees blooming for your pleasure,
You are home.

Touch your things.
View the faces smiling out at you
From frames that have been dusted.
Windows sparkle,
Furniture gleams,
Order is all around you,
Your home has been prepared for your arrival.

Walk from room to room.
Your mind is not at rest.
Planning for the new additions in your luggage,
Always planning, always thinking,
Never at rest, must have a plan.
But,

I have just returned home!

I wonder at the word "home".
Does it mean your possessions alone
Or, is home a state of mind?
Can you be at home when you are away?
Can you carry home with you?
When does home become singularly yours?
I know,

When your grief becomes tolerable.

Your home can be touched,
Your things.
Your home can be walked through and seen,
Your things.
Your desk, your comings, your goings,
Your life.

They are your home, they are you.
They are not shared today.
Today you are just one.

You are your home.
Take it on a journey,
Take it with you,
For you make up that which is home,
To you.

It is a lonely place, your home,
Unless you wrap yourself in a warm cloak,
Take your thoughts to heart,
Hear your feelings,
Understand your needs,
Come to terms with your wants,
Understand yourself
And,

Then, you will always be at home.

## Chapter XVII
## The Wander Lust is Subsiding

It was a beautiful morning for my walk on Greenwich Point, Greenwich, Connecticut. I was feeling wonderful as I enjoyed my morning constitutional! Turning onto a path I found myself behind two people. The older woman was meandering with a sweater tied around her ample middle and talking about the birds flying overhead and the wild flowers to her right. Her words and gestures were lost on her companion. Her son was five paces in front of her and not walking with her nor listening to her. It left me so sad. Wanting to shake him and encourage her was my desire. Knowing I could not, I returned home to write: **Walk With Me.**

The accompanying picture is one I have cherished. My two sons are walking away from my camera holding their small children by the hands. Remembering my childhood and wanting never to walk alone physically or mentally is so evident in this piece. Knowing my sons will walk with their children made me so happy. Can you feel my enthusiasm as "I walk my walk"?

*Joseph A. Cabrera with daughters, Brooke and Katie.*
*James P. Cabrera with sons, Peter and Jake.*

## Walk With Me

Mom and Dad, wait for me.
I just stopped to check a glitter.
Hold my hand,
Don't walk so fast.
Listen to my babbling.
Just walk with me.

I now don't have time to walk slowly,
I must walk fast.
From place to place
From experience to experience
From adventure to adventure
I am enjoying my walk.

My legs have become full grown.
My stride is full,
My mind is growing.
Walk with me as I explore.
Walk with me when I do not know.
Help me over the bridges I have not crossed.
Enlighten me with your knowledge,
Share with me, walk with me.

It is my turn to walk slower,
Their steps are guarded,
They have grown older.
I will hold their hands, their dignity,
As we travel this last road together.
I remember your heeding my request,
I will walk with you.

Saying, "good bye" was difficult,
Walking along side you both, not so.
My babble quieted as I listened,
Learning more than a book could share.
Enjoying my time,
Walking with you both.

My walk today is still brisk.
That will not always be.
There will be a day of just strolling,
Come, dear sons, walk with me.
Listen to my reminiscing,
Listen to my sense of nature,
Listen to how I love you,
As we walk together.
Walk with me.

Even when I walk alone
It is with another.
The spirit of those past
My memories accompany me.
When those memories dull,
And my company not walkable,
My walk will be with another.

For

You never walk alone.
Someone always walks with you.

## Chapter XVIII
## Me

I have wandered near and far in this second book: *Wanderings: The Continuation Of My Journey.* My body and mind have exhausted themselves as I traveled. It is a healthy tiredness as I experience life and share that with you, dear reader. In my poetry I can be found on the zephyrs of remembering, reaching for friendship, listening for the sound of a familiar voice or enjoying the essence of the day. It all has to do with that person called: me. **I Was, I Am, I Will Be** are the refrains hummed as the wind pushes me to see and hear all that surrounds me until there is not a breeze left in my world to make that next walk enjoyable. I have found the core of my existence: **me**. Sharing me with those I love and those who read my work is all important. Thank you!

*Helen M. Cabrera*

Summer 2005

120

### I Was, I Am, I Will Be

There was a time
A time when life began.
I was born, I was young,
I belonged to them.
I was their daughter.

Nurtured as I was,
I became who I am.
A part of them
A part of me, I will always be.
Ready to grow.

Every day more was added.
From every corner came newness.
Learning who and what I am
Tended by love and concern
I am.

Then one day I am was not enough.
Telling who I was became paramount.
The past become the future on my tongue.
Even the accomplishments sounded of yesterday.
I am, I was:  the wrong tense.

I wanted the future:
I Will Be.
No longer what was,
Only what could be.
A joy of holding onto yesterday,
The thrill of finding a tomorrow.

I was, I am and I Will Be!

*Write about the hope you will find in your tomorrows*